MARTIAL ART BASICS

judo

ROGER MARKS
Black belt 4th Dan

Technical consultant
AKINORI HOSAKA
Kodokan 8th Dan

Grange
BOOKS

*I acknowledge my eternal debt to my first teacher Richard Bowen,
and to Masutaro Otani, whose memory continues to inspire me.*

PLEASE NOTE:
Judo is a dynamic full-body-contact activity and there is an inherent risk of injury.
Breakfalls and partnered techniques including throws, joint locks and strangles
should only be practised in a suitable environment and under the supervision
of a qualified instructor. If you are in any doubt about your level of health
and fitness, please seek medical consultation before attempting any
of the techniques described in this book.

Published in 2008 by Grange Books
an imprint of Grange Books Ltd
35 Riverside, Sir Thomas Longley Road,
Medway City Estate, Rochester,
Kent ME2 4DP
www.grangebooks.co.uk

British Library Cataloguing-in-Publication data available on request.

ISBN 978-1-84804-021-2

1   3   5   7   9   10   8   6   4   2

AN EDDISON•SADD EDITION
Edited, designed and produced by
Eddison Sadd Editions Limited
St Chad's House, 148 King's Cross Road
London WC1X 9DH
www.eddisonsadd.com

The text and illustrations in *Martial Art Basics: Judo* were previously published
in card deck form in 2006 by Connections Book Publishing (UK),
Barnes & Noble Books (US) and Gary Allen (Aus).

Phototypeset in Zurich using QuarkXPress on Apple Macintosh

Printed in Singapore

Luton Sixth Form
ders Hill d

MARTIAL ART BASICS

judo

CONTENTS

INTRODUCTION

Why Judo?

Practised in almost every country around the world, Judo is an Olympic sport with internationally recognized rules and regulations. There are divisions suited to people of all ages and sizes, and opportunities for those with a range of disabilities to compete at all levels.

Judo is a great recreational activity and a superb way to get fit. The techniques used in Judo follow the body's natural movements, leading to the balanced development of the body, good posture, exceptional flexibility and improved stamina. The huge variety of techniques on offer means that you will never stop learning and enjoying Judo.

The strong moral and educational conventions of *Kodokan* Judo – as set down by the founder, Jigoro Kano – form the foundations of most kinds of modern Judo. Sports Judo contains the same basic principles but the emphasis is on winning competitions.

Judo philosophy

People often take up Judo purely as a hobby or to improve their fitness, and have little interest in its life-enhancing possibilities. However, Judo should be enjoyed as a true holistic experience, and, in order to build a good understanding of this martial art, there are a number of different elements that should be considered. These are:

- Physical development
- Spiritual development
- Mental development
- Contest proficiency.

Judo is essentially for the benefit of the individual, for personal development, but with the underlying concept of 'mutual benefit': you need the respect and cooperation of your fellow students to help you on the path to your personal best, and, likewise, they need you for their journey.

History

In the West, our sports and pastimes are not often linked to practical applications, usually bearing only the slightest relationship to 'real life'. In Japan, Judo was developed and derived from martial arts that were refined to the highest degree at the time of the Samurai, the warrior caste. Before a battle, a champion from each army would engage in combat, usually ending in the death of one of them. If the result was judged to be fair, the two armies would not engage in battle, sparing many soldiers' lives. This ideal of the individual achieving personal martial arts skills for the benefit of others and to bring about peace is reflected in modern *budo*, the Japanese martial arts-derived activities that include Judo, Aikido, Kendo and Karate, among many others.

Practical matters

Once you've made the decision to take up Judo, there are a few issues to consider.

Choosing a club

Contact your national Judo body for details of the registered coaches and clubs in your area. Try to sit in on a few training sessions to gain an idea of whether the teaching style and club ethos would suit you. Speak to the teacher and some of the club members. Some places run special induction courses for beginners, which can be useful. Will the session times and location allow you to commit to a regular training regime?

Your teacher should have a grade that is recognized by a national Judo body and be fully insured to teach. Although reaching Dan grade (black belt) level should indicate a sound basic knowledge and experience of Judo, it doesn't necessarily indicate good teaching skills, so find out if they hold any nationally recognized teaching qualifications. It's also important to note whether they are safety aware.

Getting a licence

When you start learning Judo, you should join the national Judo body that your club is affiliated to. You will be given a licence, which acts as a record of your Judo career, eventually including details of your grade assessments, competition attendance and results, and other information relating to courses completed at regional, national and international level. It will also note any related qualifications such as first aid, teaching and refereeing. The licence should include an element of personal insurance covering some of the eventualities not relevant to the instructor's liability insurance.

The reputable organizations that issue licences exist for the benefit of their members. They also fulfill other roles:

- Setting the technical standards and issuing a syllabus for their members' development and grade assessments
- Establishing codes of behaviour for members and teachers
- Operating a training scheme for teachers and

assistant teachers at club and national level
- Keeping their members up to date with news and details of courses, competitions and grade assessments.

Once inside the dojo

In a typical adult session there will be students of all ages and a whole range of grades taking part. The teaching methods for children should be modified to suit their stage of development, and most Judo clubs will offer separate sessions for children, often dividing them up into primary and junior age groups. However, it is possible that the more experienced and physically developed juniors will be invited to take part in sessions for adults.

Preparing to start

In Judo, as in all martial arts, etiquette plays a very important part. From the moment you step inside the *dojo* (practice hall), a code of practice should be adhered to.

As you enter the dojo it's customary to make a standing bow towards the position designated the *joza* (upper seat), where the higher grades sit on formal occasions. In some clubs it is expected that shoes are removed before entering and are left outside the dojo.

Plan to arrive at the class early to allow time to register, get changed into your judogi and, if necessary, help with cleaning the dojo and laying the *tatami* (mats).

At the edge of the mat, remove your shoes (flip-flops or similar) and leave them by the side of the mat with the toes facing outwards. Facing the mat, stand with your feet together and make a standing bow before stepping onto the mat. No footwear (including socks) is worn on the mat.

Tying the obi

Putting on your *judogi* (Judo suit) and tying the *obi* (belt) takes practice. These tips should help.

Hold the belt in the centre.

Place the middle of the belt on the lower abdomen and wrap around the body.

Bring the lower end across the body, thread the other end through the gap, and pull up to make a reef knot.

Fasten the belt as if tying the beginning of a bow. Once pulled through, the ends should be equal in length.

Students line up along one side of the mat in grade order, beginners on the left, and face the *sensei* (the teacher and any black belts who are present). On command of *seiza* (meaning 'be seated'), all students bow to the sensei.

The bow

From a standing position, place the left and then right knee on the mat. Your knees should be two hand widths apart. Move your toes back so that the tops of your feet are flat on the mat. The big toes should be almost overlapping. Then lower the body into

the final position, seiza, resting the buttocks in the 'V' formed by the heels. Keep your back straight.

On the command *rei* ('bow'), place your hands on the mat – palms down, fingers together – with your elbows bent outwards. Bow with the sensei by lowering your body forwards. Bow only for a few seconds, then return to seiza. The bow is made with respect and concentration .

The instructor may wish to make a few points about the session; remain in seiza until requested to stand. To return to standing, reverse the sitting procedure.

2 **Cardiovascular** Try star jumps, running around the mat – anything that increases the heart rate and breathing rate.

3 **Flexibility and stretching** See the stretching exercises on pages 16–17.

4 **Strength** Press-ups and squat-thrusts are ideal for helping to build strength.

5 **Judo-specific** See the exercises shown on pages 18–21. It's vital to include breakfall exercises as they will help to prepare you for the following session. Other exercises will be chosen according to the technical content of the class.

Learning and practising techniques

The techniques demonstrated in a session will be chosen according to the standard of the students in the group. The instructor will make sure there is something suitable for everyone to work on. Beginners and lower grades will practise at their own level, but will have the opportunity to benefit from the experience of higher grades.

Methods of practice include:

- *Uchikomi* Multirepetition training that allows the body to learn movements correctly.
- *Randori* Similar to sparring in boxing, where partners experiment with techniques, helping each other to improve. Variations may include 'throw-for-throw', where partners take it in turns to apply a technique skilfully while moving. Although you shouldn't resist your partner too much, it's important not to allow poor techniques to succeed. Students should always focus on applying a technique safely, and their partner's ability to receive it without injury.
- *Shiai* This is a contest under contest rules, with a win, lose or draw outcome.

Pull tightly to secure, ensuring the ends are of equal length.

When you release the ends they should both hang downwards!

Warming up

A warming-up routine is essential to increase the heart rate, depth of breathing and metabolic rate. In addition, muscles and body joints are less prone to damage when they're warm. You should also benefit from quicker reaction times and enhanced mental alertness.

The time, intensity and specific exercises used will depend on the length of the session and the fitness level of the group. But this warm-up sequence will give you an idea.

1 **Loosening joints** It's useful to work first on the neck, then move to the arms, shoulders and wrists, and then the spine, hips, knees, ankles and toes. See the Warming Up section on pages 14–21.

● *Kata* Translated as 'form', this is a partnered formal demonstration of the principles of Judo and, although usually performed by higher grades, has great value as a training aid for those seeking to perfect their Judo. There are many *kata*, some of which seek to preserve the technical origins of Judo, including working with weapons.

Ending the session

A Judo session can be very physically demanding, and cooling-down exercises are important to bring the body and mind back to a normal state. This will minimize the discomfort and stiffness that can follow a hard workout! The Stretching exercises shown in the Warming Up section are ideal for this purpose. It's also a good idea to do a few breathing exercises before you finish.

After cooling down, the session will be formally ended. Like the start of the class, this involves lining up and bowing. If your instructor has anything to say about the practice or club notices to give out, this will take place before you are dismissed. If required, help to clean the dojo and store the mats before leaving. Remember to bow when exiting.

About this book

This book is designed to give you a good understanding of the basic Judo skills. It's not intended to take the place of an instructor, but will provide an invaluable resource to kick-start your Judo experience and aid your progress. Don't feel that you have to work through the book in the order in which it's set out. Simply turn to the pages that relate to the aspect of your technique that you're focusing on at any given time.

Some of the breakfall exercises shown can be practised outside the class, but a full breakfall from a standing position belongs in the dojo. Likewise, any of the throws, joint locks and strangles should be practised in the presence of a qualified instructor, in a suitable environment.

Making the grade

Once you're familiar with the fundamentals of basic Judo and are confident in your ability to do breakfalls, you will work towards your first grade assessments. In the larger clubs, grading for up to green belt may take place within the club itself. Smaller clubs may arrange their gradings with other clubs belonging to the same Judo body, or their students can visit a larger club to take their assessment.

The syllabus for grade requirements varies from one Judo body to another, but, for your first few grades, emphasis will be placed on basic techniques and your ability to practise safely. You will also be required to demonstrate good etiquette and an understanding of basic rules and vocabulary. Your assessment may also include some *randori* (free practice) or *shiai* (contest), to assess how well you're mastering breakfalls and other fundamental principles. Standards of behaviour are also noted.

Once green-belt standard has been reached, most Judo organizations require students to demonstrate their contest ability against others of the same grade. If, because of your age or a disability, it's considered that you shouldn't contest for your grade, alternatives will be offered. Teaching or refereeing experience, or other services you offer your club or organization, may be recognized by advancement in grade.

Assessments for the higher *kyu* grades (steps towards black belt) and recommendations for Dan grades usually take place at designated events away from the club.

Grading systems

Grades are denoted by the colour of the belt. Although the number of kyu grades and the colours of the belts may vary from one organization to another, most use a version of the following system. Note that 1st kyu is the *highest* kyu grade whereas 1st Dan is the *lowest* Dan grade.

Kyu grades

6th kyu *white*	●	3rd kyu *green*
5th kyu *yellow*	●	2nd kyu *blue*
4th kyu *orange*	●	1st kyu *brown*

Dan grades

1st–5th Dan *black*
6th–8th Dan *red/white blocks*
9th–10th Dan *red*

Primary grades (for young children) are usually indicated by a system of coloured stripes on a white belt. This allows for a large number of increments so young students can move through the grades quickly. This really helps to boost their sense of achievement. Juniors (older children) have a similar system, with the stripes being combined with coloured belts to differentiate junior grades from primary.

Most Judo organizations do not grade children as a senior black belt (Dan grade) apart from in a few exceptional cases; it's accepted that not many children would be able to hold their own in a contest with an adult. When junior grades reach the age to be designated as seniors, they can then work towards obtaining a senior grade.

What next?

When you've been learning Judo for perhaps six months or so and have worked towards your first (successful!) grading, you may have a good idea of the huge range of possibilities that Judo can offer.

You might be happy to carry on practising for fun and/or physical fitness, and be content with your once- or twice-weekly sessions. You'll join other members of your club on occasional visits to other local clubs, take part in low-key competitions, and support your club in any major competitions.

Or, you might catch the Judo bug big time! You will take every opportunity to practise and work towards your next grade, as well as going to as many other clubs and courses as you can, entering competitions and meeting Judo enthusiasts all over the country and abroad, bringing your experiences back to help inspire the other members of your club.

If you have the ambition and potential to become a Judo champion, your teacher, club and Judo organization will advise you and help you select a coach who will work with you to organize your development and enable you to reach your goals.

Do the best you can, be safe and have fun!

WARMING UP

Mobility

A warm-up should always begin with gentle stretches and flexibility exercises. The range and intensity can be increased as the body adjusts. Work on the neck first, then move down the body making sure no area is missed out. These exercises can also be used in the cooling-down routine.

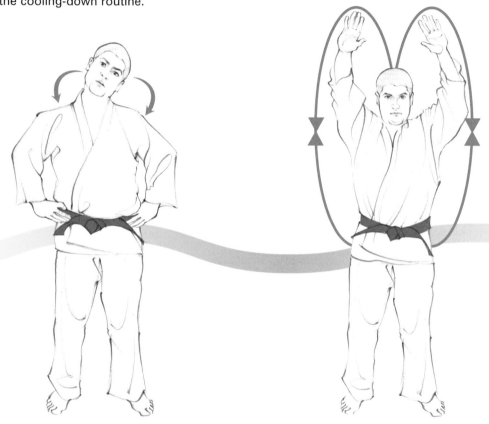

▲ NECK TURNS Place your hands on your hips, and slowly turn your head to one side, then the other. Next, lean your head forwards and then backwards – look ahead rather than directly upwards. One at a time, lower the ears to the shoulders as shown. Then, taking great care, slowly rotate the head so that it traces a forward-facing semicircle – don't allow your head to lean backwards.

▲ SHOULDER MOVES Short-range movements of the shoulder joints, such as shrugs and rotations with the arms by the sides, can be followed by larger-range actions with the arms extended – for example, forward and reverse arm rotations, and 'windmills', changing direction several times and gradually increasing the speed.

WARNING
Take care when exercising the neck as the weight of the head can cause an injury such as whiplash. To avoid this, always move the head and neck very slowly.

▶ ANKLE BENDS There are many throwing techniques in Judo that require good ankle flexibility. For this exercise, put one foot forward, bend the ankle to flex the toes and rest the heel on the mat, then lift the heel and point the toes downwards. Repeat several times before changing to the other ankle.

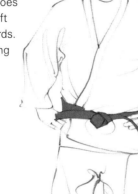

Pointed toes
(detail)

▼ HIP ROTATIONS Strong, flexible hips are important for nearly all Judo techniques. With the hands on the hips, rotate the hips in large circular movements, keeping the head as still as possible. Repeat in the other direction. Then, from the same position, move the hips from side to side, then from front to back. Repeat several times.

◀ KNEE BENDS From a standing position, bend forwards from the hips, then place a hand on each kneecap and squat down. Pushing gently on the kneecaps, rise up to stand. This exercise should be done slowly and steadily. Don't bounce.

Stretching

Good flexibility is very important if you want to become proficient at Judo. The following exercises will help. Always stretch slowly and hold each position for about 10 seconds. Do not bounce. These moves can also be used as part of the cooling-down process, when the duration and range of movement can be extended.

> **WARNING**
> **Stretching should only be carried out after the soft tissues have been warmed up sufficiently with cardiovascular exercise.**

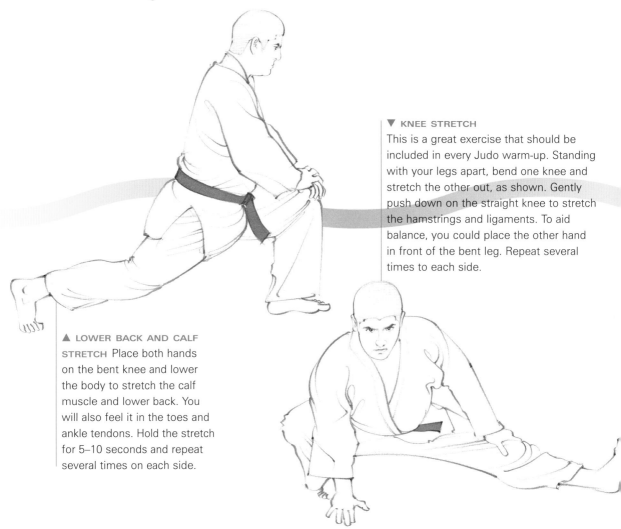

▼ KNEE STRETCH

This is a great exercise that should be included in every Judo warm-up. Standing with your legs apart, bend one knee and stretch the other out, as shown. Gently push down on the straight knee to stretch the hamstrings and ligaments. To aid balance, you could place the other hand in front of the bent leg. Repeat several times to each side.

▲ LOWER BACK AND CALF STRETCH Place both hands on the bent knee and lower the body to stretch the calf muscle and lower back. You will also feel it in the toes and ankle tendons. Hold the stretch for 5–10 seconds and repeat several times on each side.

BACK STRETCH

1◄ This is an excellent exercise for Judo that, when done slowly and with full extension, promotes trunk and shoulder flexibility and improves balance. Note the posture: the arms are stretched behind the back; the hips are pushed forwards slightly to retain balance, and this also helps to create the deep backward bend. Hold this posture briefly before moving on to step 2.

2▶ Slowly stand upright, then bend forwards and down, pushing your hands through your open legs as far as you can manage. Repeat steps 1 and 2 five to ten times.

▶ BACK BEND This is the well-known Yogic 'Cobra' pose; it has a very powerful effect on the back. Start by lying flat with your hands underneath your shoulders. Then push up, keeping the hips down. Your legs should be a short distance apart and your toes push into the mat to grip – this is important for your groundwork. Keep your arms straight to hold the body in position, but relax your shoulders. Hold this position for a short while.

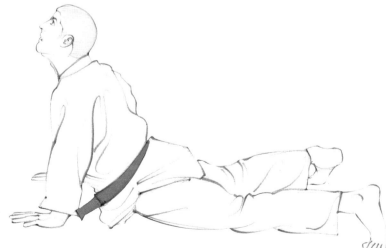

Judo-specific exercises (1)

Judo-specific exercises are designed to help you improve your coordination, flexibility, core strength and body management – all skills that aid the overall development of the Judo student. They also help you to concentrate on certain technical aspects of Judo. These moves provide particularly good preparation for the groundwork grappling techniques.

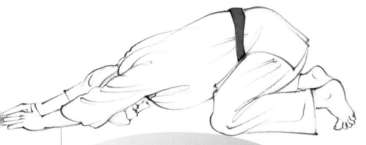

▲ CAT STRETCH On all fours, slide your arms forwards while lowering the body. As you extend your arms you should feel the effect on the shoulder, back and hip muscles. Hold this position for 10 seconds. The cat stretch is also useful for cooling down, when the pose may be held for longer.

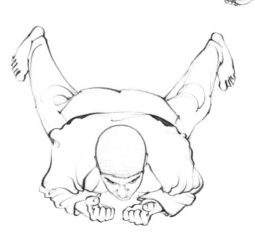

▶ GRIP PULLS Lie on your front with your legs apart and toes pointing down. Your arms should be stretched out in front of you, palms facing up. Clench your fists and pull strongly with your arms and upper body only, to slide yourself forwards. Keep your hips on the mat. Then stretch your arms out again and repeat. Aim to travel to the other end of the mat. This is a strenuous exercise but it's excellent for developing good grip and strong, flexible wrists, which are important for the upper-four-quarters hold (*see pages 62–3*).

TOP TIP
When performing a Judo-specific exercise, visualize the techniques that the movements relate to and focus on the dynamic nature of the action. Accuracy of the movement is important.

THE SNAKE

1◄ This is a complex exercise. Don't be discouraged if initial attempts are compared to a flopping fish stranded on dry land! The sequence has two modes: head first and feet first. This is the easier head-first method. Start with your head up, hands raised and feet on the mat.

2◄ Turn your body to the right while bringing your right knee towards your chest and drawing your right heel towards the buttocks.

5▲ Bringing your left foot towards your buttocks, push with your left leg and straighten up. Repeat the sequence until you reach the end of the mat.

4▲ You should now have returned to the start position. Rotate your body to the left and push down with your hands while bringing your upper body down towards your middle.

3◄ Push with your right leg to straighten out the body, as you start to lean over to your left. Move yourself forwards by coordinating the push from the feet with the movement of the body.

Judo-specific exercises (2)

Judo-specific exercises should not be treated as a substitute for practising with a partner – to learn Judo you must *practise* Judo.

▲ BODY DROP JUMPS
Standing upright with your weight evenly distributed, bend your knees and jump into the position shown. Note the grip of the hands. Practise the move to both sides, extending your movement as you improve by turning through 90 degrees, 180 degrees and finally 360 degrees! Concentrate on maintaining the form. This stance is used to form the final position of body drop throw (*see pages 38–9*).

▶ FIST SNAPS
In a standing position, lift your arms to shoulder height and bend the wrists so your fingers point down. Snap your wrists up sharply and clench the fists. Repeat rapidly with power, building up to high repetitions. This will improve the speed and effectiveness of taking grip – a vital contest skill.

▲ Clenched fists (detail)

▶ LEG KICKS
Lie on your back with your head raised and your hands under your hips. Keeping your legs off the ground, kick with alternate legs, heels forward. This will develop your leg flexibility and power in preparation for groundwork.

LEG SWEEPS

1◀ You'll need to be near a wall for this. Stand facing the wall with your feet parallel and apart. Place both hands on the wall for support. Turning your hips anticlockwise, step forwards and out to the left with your right foot and bring the left leg behind, so that you stand side-on to the wall.

2▼ In an energetic combined movement, swing the inner leg up and straighten the outer leg. To achieve the correct final position, your head, body and leg should form a straight line. Practise several times to each side. This move is used in the inner-thigh throw (*see pages 42–3*).

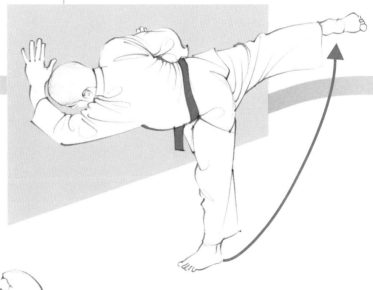

TOP TIP
When practising leg sweeps, keep the sweeping leg straight to develop speed and power in a full-range, extended sweeping movement.

BREAKFALLS

Back breakfall
Ushiro ukemi

Practising breakfall techniques (ukemi waza) regularly will give you the confidence required to develop your Judo skilfully. Breakfalls should become an instinctive reaction to being thrown, reducing the chances of injury.

2▲ As your body rolls backwards, keep your chin tucked into the chest to maintain a rounded back and prevent your head from slapping the mat. The momentum will bring your legs over your head.

3▼ Bring your hands down sharply – arms at 30–45 degrees to the body – so that the palms slap the mat. Avoid straining the shoulders. Bring your hands back in front of your face, wrists crossed. Swing your legs forwards and down to the mat, and return to standing using the forward momentum.

1▲ Bend your knees and balance on your toes with your arms straight out in front of you. With your fingers together and palms facing outwards, cross your wrists. Then tuck your chin into your chest and, with your back slightly rounded, start to fall backwards.

Side breakfall
Yoko ukemi

The side breakfall is the most regularly used of all the breakfall techniques and should be practised to both sides.

1 ▶ Sweep your left arm and leg across the body while bending the supporting leg. Your body will start to drop towards the left.

TOP TIP
The hand should contact the mat with a percussive slap rather than a rigid, hard blow, so that the recoil can be used to bring the hands to the final position.

2 ▶ Continue to sweep your leg across and bend the knee of the supporting leg. The sweeping leg will contact the mat and your body will fall to the side.

3 ▶ As the body makes contact with the floor, slap the mat with your palm, fingers together and arm at around 30–45 degrees to the body. Open your legs wide – the outside of your left foot, the inside of your right, and the tip of your shoulder provide support for the rest of your body, and protect your back and hips. Your hand recoils back to cover your face. Repeat to the right-hand side.

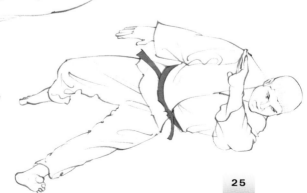

Rolling breakfall
Jenpo kaiten ukemi

The rolling breakfall can dissipate a lot of kinetic energy and there are some dynamic throwing techniques that will require this.

1▲ From standing, slide one foot forward, place your fingertips together as shown, and bend the front knee. Turn your head to look through your arms towards your rear leg.

TOP TIP
Practising the front and rolling breakfalls from standing can be intimidating, so to begin with start on your knees. Gradually work towards achieving a fully upright position.

WARNING
When practising the rolling breakfall, do not roll over your head as this could damage the head and neck. The correct technique is to roll over one shoulder; the arm is used to guide the body over without your head touching the mat.

4▶ The final position is that of the side breakfall; slap the mat and recoil with the hand that led the movement. As you gain skill, practise the roll at higher speeds. Eventually, you should build up enough momentum to finish the move standing up. Practise to both sides.

Front breakfall
Mai ukemi

2◀ Still looking at the rear leg, rest your hands on the mat just inside the front foot. Bend the rear leg slightly and then push forwards over the outside arm and shoulder, creating impetus by raising the rear heel and straightening the knee.

The front breakfall is used to protect against serious facial damage should your partner have insufficient control to make you fall on your back, or if you attempt to spoil the technique by twisting out.

3▼ The body continues to rotate forwards over the front arm – which acts as a wheel rim – making a diagonal, circular movement from front hand to rear heel.

1▲ Starting from standing, bend your knees and fall forwards, raising your forearms in front of you as you drop.

2▲ Contact the mat with the whole length of your forearms – from elbow to fingertips – absorbing the impact. Your legs should spring apart with the pads of your toes taking your weight. The knees and hips are lifted away from the mat.

STANDING JUDO

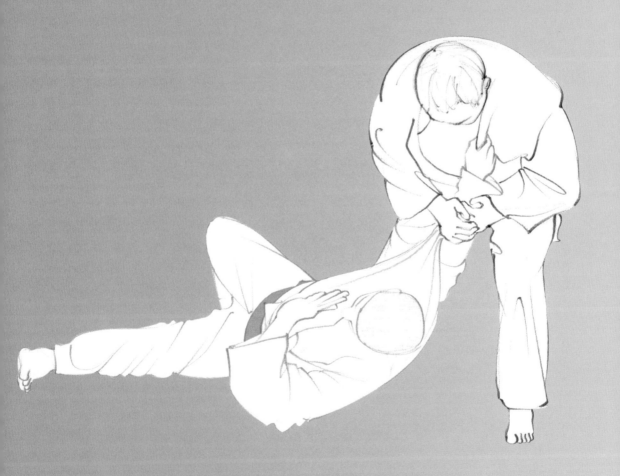

Posture

There are certain rules concerning posture and moving around the mat, that must be learned and strictly adhered to if you are to become a skilled Judo practitioner. Take care not to develop bad habits, as these can be hard to break and will slow your progress.

1▼ This is the basic natural posture (shizen hon tai). Stand with your feet about shoulder width apart, and your toes pointing outwards slightly. You should feel perfectly balanced and relaxed with your weight on the balls of your feet, ready to move in any direction.

2◄ From the natural standing position, move into right natural posture (migi shizentai) by sliding your right foot forwards or left foot back. Turn the right foot in slightly and the left out about 90 degrees. This relaxed, balanced stance allows for quick, smooth movement when holding your opponent. For left natural posture (hidari shizentai), follow these instructions but switch left and right.

3► When your opponent attempts an attack, you may defend by moving into defensive posture (jigotai). Bend your knees and widen your stance to lower your hips and centre of gravity.

Moving

1◄ The feet rarely pass each other. Move forwards by stepping with one foot and then following with the other so that the toes are almost level with the heel of the first. This is done with the feet just lifting off the mat (sugi ashi) or with a sliding action (suri ashi).

TOP TIP
If you need to change from natural to defensive posture, move back to a natural stance as soon as you can so that you are in a strong position should you wish to attack.

2► To move backwards, slide the rear foot back with the same action as moving forwards, transferring your weight to it. Bring your front foot back until the heel is almost in line with the toes of your back foot. To progress backwards, repeat.

3► With your partner, practise moving forwards, backwards, sideways and in a circle, never letting the feet pass each other. This image shows a turning movement, with a pull on the collar to bring the receiver around. Keep one foot in position to act as a pivot.

Starting your practice

The correct behaviour should always be observed during a Judo session, however formal or informal the circumstances. The following sequence demonstrates how a contest (*shiai*) or standing free practice (*randori*) progresses. Note that in a contest you would always start 6 ft (1.75 m) away from your partner to make your preliminary bow.

2▼ Stand upright again and take a full step forwards with the left leg then the right, to stand in basic natural posture with your feet parallel and shoulder width apart. This is the start position.

1▲ Before standing partner practice, a technique demonstration or a contest, stand facing your partner, your hands on the sides of your thighs and feet together. Bow simultaneously, bending from the hips to about 30 degrees.

TOP TIP
Keep your partner within your peripheral vision when bowing; don't let your guard drop – even for a moment!

4▼ Spar with your partner until you hear the command of *'Matte!'* (stop). Immediately return to the start position and stand in basic natural posture. In a contest situation after the score is given, step back, right foot followed by left, and bow (see step 1). Always show your respect for your partner by bowing at the end of your practice.

3▲ On command of *'Hajime!'* (start), immediately step forwards and take your grip in natural posture. Preferably, take hold of the collar with one hand and control the sleeve, by holding just above the elbow, with the other. In general practice, partners tend to take symmetrical holds; it's good practice to first control the sleeve, then the collar.

THROWS

Double-handed shoulder throw
Morote seoinage

Double-handed shoulder throw is one of a range of shoulder throws, or back-carry throws (seoinage), favoured by smaller people – to execute the technique, the shoulder is placed under the armpit of the receiver (*uke*).

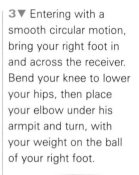

3▼ Entering with a smooth circular motion, bring your right foot in and across the receiver. Bend your knee to lower your hips, then place your elbow under his armpit and turn, with your weight on the ball of your right foot.

1▲ Standing side-on to your opponent with your and his feet forming a 'T', grip high on his collar and drop your weight towards your rear leg. Use your wrists to draw your partner down and forwards to disturb his forward balance.

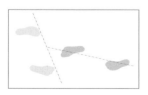

2▲ Lift your opponent's body and open out your elbows. This will work with step 1 to make the receiver straighten up and become unbalanced so that he tilts forwards with his weight shifted to his toes.

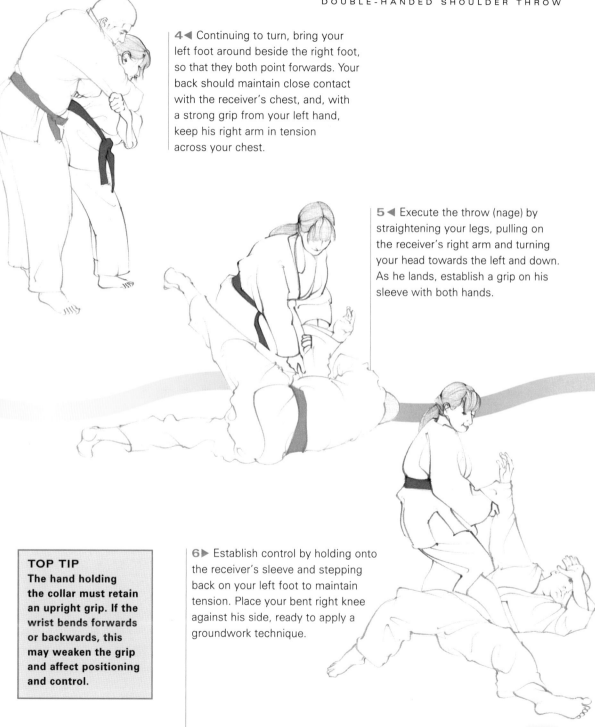

4◀ Continuing to turn, bring your left foot around beside the right foot, so that they both point forwards. Your back should maintain close contact with the receiver's chest, and, with a strong grip from your left hand, keep his right arm in tension across your chest.

5◀ Execute the throw (nage) by straightening your legs, pulling on the receiver's right arm and turning your head towards the left and down. As he lands, establish a grip on his sleeve with both hands.

TOP TIP
The hand holding the collar must retain an upright grip. If the wrist bends forwards or backwards, this may weaken the grip and affect positioning and control.

6▶ Establish control by holding onto the receiver's sleeve and stepping back on your left foot to maintain tension. Place your bent right knee against his side, ready to apply a groundwork technique.

Body drop throw
Tai otoshi

Body drop throw is a hand throw with no hip contact. Relying on speed and momentum, it can be used effectively by small, light students against opponents of any size and physical type.

1▲ Stand side-on to your opponent so that the two pairs of feet are in the 'T' position (*see page 36*). Take a high-collar grip on his lapel and slide your rear foot back, transferring some of your weight onto it. At the same time, disturb the receiver's posture and balance by pulling down with both hands.

2▲ Move your hips towards the receiver as you pull your hands up and your elbows outwards to make space for entering. The receiver is straightened up on his toes with his balance broken to the front.

3◄ Place your forearm against your partner's chest and push upwards, bringing your outside leg behind you as you do so. Turning your body clockwise, pull his right arm with your left hand and bring his head and shoulders around with your right.

> **TOP TIP**
> In steps 3 and 4, don't take your outside foot too far back. The final position of the foot must be far enough forward of the receiver's left foot for you to be able to keep your balance and maintain the momentum of the throw.

4► Move your right foot across so that it almost touches that of the receiver. Bend your knees and place your legs wide apart with your weight evenly distributed. Complete the throw by pulling with your left hand and pushing with your right, to guide the receiver. To assist this move, turn to the left and spring up with your legs.

Foot positioning (detail)

5► Maintain control by holding your partner's right sleeve and keeping tension in his arm. This assists him with the breakfall and leaves you with the initiative, allowing for continuation into groundwork.

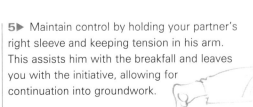

Shoulder drop throw
Seoi otoshi

Shoulder drop throw combines elements of double-handed shoulder throw and body drop throw. There are several versions of this technique, some nearer to a shoulder throw and others closer to a body drop throw in appearance. The one shown here is the latter.

3▲ Bring your right elbow across the receiver's chest and into his right armpit, which will have opened up.

1▲ Standing side-on to your partner, the two pairs of feet forming a 'T' (*see page 36*), take a small step back and grip high on his collar. Drop your weight onto your back foot and bring your opponent down, pulling his upper body forwards and breaking his posture.

2▶ Bring your front leg forwards and straighten your opponent up onto his toes. Pull your elbows outwards to create a space for the entry, keeping the receiver off-balance to the front.

4▲ Swivel on the balls of your feet and move your right leg across to bring you into a wide-knees, bent stance with your foot in front of your opponent's ankle.

5▶ To execute the throw, turn your head and hips while pulling strongly with both hands in a downward, diagonal motion.

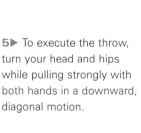

6▲ Once you've thrown your opponent, make sure you maintain good posture, control and body contact, and keep hold of his arm with both hands to retain tension, ready to enter into groundwork.

TOP TIP
Keep the receiver unbalanced throughout the execution of the technique. Don't pull him forwards or let him drop his weight back, as either action will give him a chance to recover his balance.

Inner-thigh throw
Uchi mata

Inner-thigh throw is classified as a foot/leg technique, although it may seem similar to a hip technique if the sweeping leg is inserted deeply. Here, the person executing the technique (*tori*) sweeps the back of his thigh to contact the receiver's inner thigh. This is a useful throw to use when your opponent has adopted a wide-legged, low stance.

2◀ Using the receiver's reaction, straighten him up with both hands and take his balance forwards. Move your right foot across and into the centre, and pull on the lapel to bring his left foot forwards slightly.

1▲ Stand side-on to your partner, feet in the 'T' position (*see page 36*), and, with a high grip on his collar, pull down to unsettle him.

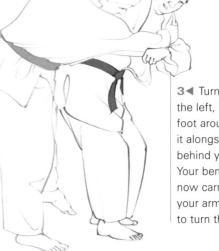

3◀ Turning your hip to the left, bring your left foot around and place it alongside and slightly behind your right foot. Your bent left leg should now carry your weight; your arms are starting to turn the receiver over.

4◄ With a vigorous sweep, drive your right leg through the receiver's legs with your upper thigh making contact with his inner thigh. Straighten your supporting leg to add impetus and turn your head and shoulders to the left. In a combined movement, pull your left arm strongly across your chest and push with your right arm, so that the receiver completes a curved fall, landing on his back.

5◄ At the moment of impact and afterwards, continue to focus on combat awareness (*zanshin*), ready to make the next move.

TOP TIP
At step 4, make sure your head, body and sweeping leg are in a straight line, with your toes pointed. This adds impetus, coordination and contact with your opponent – essential for crisp execution of the technique.

Lift pull hip throw
Tsuri komi goshi

Lift pull hip throw combines a strong pushing action of the right arm with a lift of the hips to form a powerful throw. In this example, the elbow is lifted under the receiver's armpit. This can be an effective way to deal with an opponent's attempt to go into defensive posture and avoid a hip throw.

> **TOP TIP**
> **Keep looking at the receiver as you unbalance him and make the entering movements in step 2.**

2▼ Make space to enter by drawing the receiver's elbows outwards. Move your right foot in and towards his right foot, while placing your right elbow into his left armpit. Use your left hand to pull his right arm across your upper chest.

1▲ Standing side-on to your partner, pull down on him to break his posture. This makes him unbalance forwards and brings his weight onto his toes.

3▶ To complete the entry, turn on the ball of your right foot and bring your left leg back with the toes pointing forwards, so your feet are parallel to each other. Bend both knees and keep your hips low. Make firm body contact with the receiver, who will be bent over and raised high on his toes.

4▶ To execute the throw, snap your knees straight and pull strongly with your left hand. Simultaneously, lift the receiver by the collar and turn him over your hip to land on his back.

5▶ Stay firmly balanced and in control, ready for the next move.

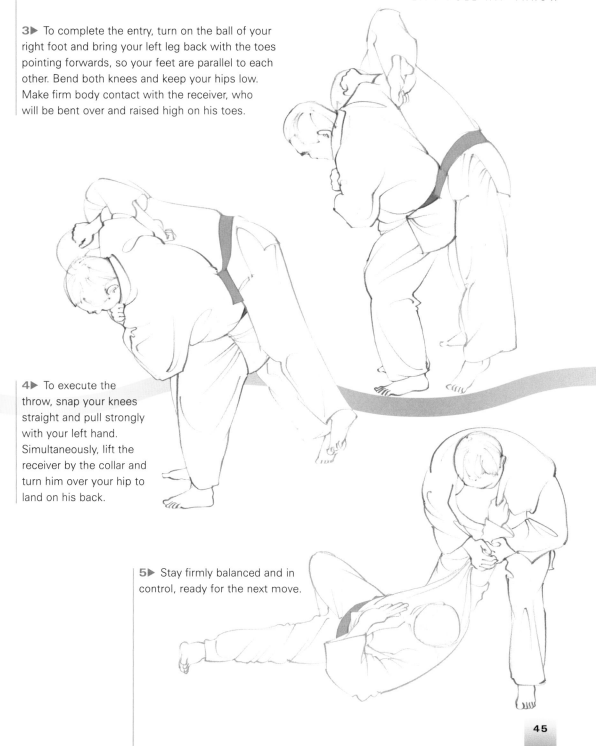

Combination (1)

Here, double-handed shoulder throw is combined with major inner reap (o uchi gari). The combination throw will vary according to the action the receiver takes to avoid the original technique. In this example, he is open to be unbalanced to his rear left, perfect for major inner reap.

1▼ As you turn in and withdraw the left foot to make full body contact for the completion of the double-handed shoulder throw, the receiver drops his hips to lower his centre of gravity and pulls away in an attempt to regain the initiative.

2▲ Immediately withdraw your arm from your opponent's armpit, turning your hips and bringing your outside foot around so that you're standing side-on to him and can look at him. Grasp his collar with your right hand to make him unbalance to the rear left.

TOP TIP
You must react immediately as your opponent drops into a defensive posture, by turning back to face him. Any hesitation will give him an opportunity to apply a counter attack.

3 ◄ To further unbalance the receiver, push backwards and downwards with your right hand. Notice the position of his head; this indicates that the balance has been taken to the rear.

4 ► Maintaining pressure to the rear, bring your outside leg towards your opponent and drive your other leg between his legs and behind the left calf. Draw your leg around in a clockwise movement with your big toe just touching the mat, and reap the receiver's left leg forwards while pushing back and down with both hands, to execute major inner reap.

5 ► Release your grip on the receiver to allow him to make a breakfall.

Combination (2)

Here, body drop throw is combined with minor inner reap (ko uchi gari). This follows the principle of a small throw being used in combination with a big throw.

1▼ Your partner manages to partially spoil your body drop throw just before completion by dropping his heels to the mat and transferring body weight backward off the right foot.

2▲ You are still maintaining the pull of the body drop throw around your body. Your partner follows this and steps around, bringing his right foot in front of yours in an attempt to avoid being thrown and regain the initiative.

3▶ Turn in to your right, taking a small step with your left foot. Use both hands to bring your partner's balance over his extended front leg. With the sole of your right foot turned inwards, make contact with his heel and lower ankle.

4▶ Execute minor inner reap by sweeping the receiver's foot in the direction of his toes, while pulling down strongly with both hands.

TOP TIP
You must react very sharply in step 4 to make sure you catch the receiver behind the heel and sweep just as he starts to transfer his weight to his right foot and place it on the mat.

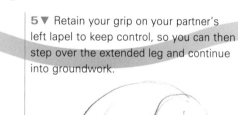

5▼ Retain your grip on your partner's left lapel to keep control, so you can then step over the extended leg and continue into groundwork.

Combination (3)

This combination of shoulder drop throw and major outer reap (o soto gari) demonstrates how to take advantage of a change of direction imposed by your opponent to force you to alter your throw.

2▼ Turn towards your opponent, and straighten your right knee to regain stability while moving your right elbow so that it loses contact with him. Use both hands to unbalance the receiver to the rear.

1▲ The receiver lowers his centre of gravity and bends his right knee to push against the back of your knee. He transfers his weight to his back leg to spoil the technique, preventing you from using the shoulder drop throw to throw him.

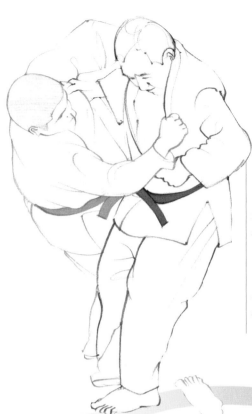

TOP TIP
If your opponent blocks a technique, rather than trying to resist it, take advantage of the action. A good tactic is to use a move that will encourage a certain reaction, setting your partner up for your planned combination technique.

3◄ Bring your left leg around and place it outside your partner's right leg. Then use your hands and body to unbalance him to the rear right. Raise your right leg and energetically reap his right leg away, your hands guiding his body back and down.

4▶ The dynamic action of major outer reap is indicated in this picture. The hands guide the body to land flat. You can continue into groundwork, but take care not to lose your balance and fall on your partner.

Combination (4)

Inner-thigh throw is here combined with minor outer reap (ko soto gari). This is an example of a minor throw being used with a major technique. Note the change of direction required by the person executing the technique.

TOP TIP
Use your right hand to take the receiver's lapel over his shoulder. Then pull down, putting his weight onto his left heel and unbalancing him to the rear.

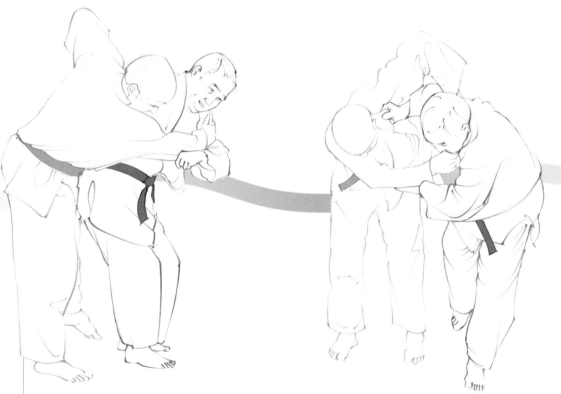

1▲ As you start the sweeping action of the inner-thigh throw, your partner manages to place his left foot on the mat, regaining some balance.

2▲ As your right foot continues to move back, your partner moves his feet sideways to get out of the path of the sweeping leg, and stands with his legs parallel. Abort your sweep by placing your right foot on the mat.

3▼ Turn to your right by swivelling on the balls of your feet, so that you face your partner's left side. Break his balance to the rear left by pushing his right elbow up and pulling his left shoulder down and back. Using the sole of your right foot, slap his left heel forward.

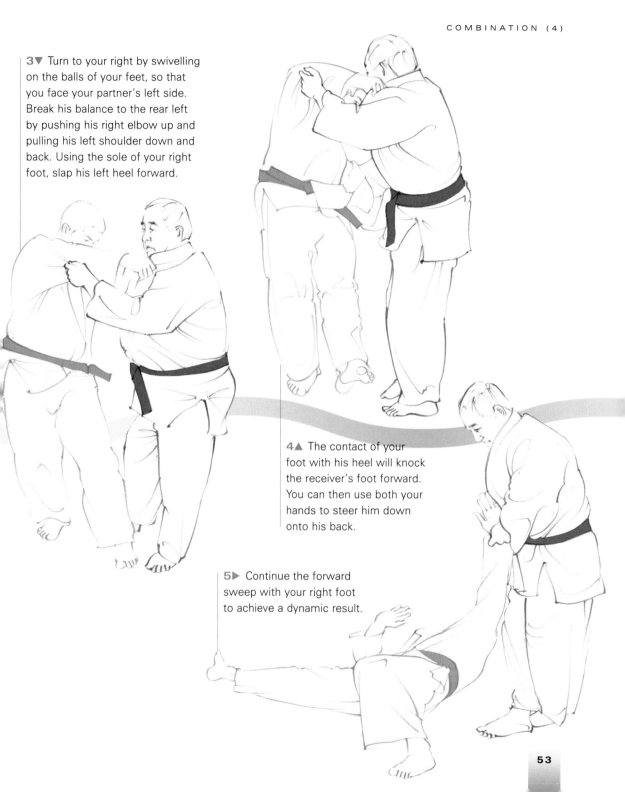

4▲ The contact of your foot with his heel will knock the receiver's foot forward. You can then use both your hands to steer him down onto his back.

5▶ Continue the forward sweep with your right foot to achieve a dynamic result.

Combination (5)

Here, lift pull hip throw is combined with a foot technique, lift pull foot (tsuri komi ashi). It demonstrates a way to regain control when the receiver has blocked your attempted hip throw but remains in a static position. By utilizing the lift-pull movement of the foot technique, you can introduce some dynamic impetus.

2▼ In response, start turning back to face your partner. As you do so, pull his lapel towards your right shoulder and turn your left shoulder in towards him.

3▲ Continue the action from step 2, now bringing your left leg around and pushing on your partner's right arm to turn his upper body to face you. Then adjust your arm movement to push his right elbow up and pull his lapel down.

1▲ As you turn in for lift pull hip throw, your partner goes into defensive posture. He keeps his head upright and partly breaks body contact to spoil your attempted throw.

4▼ Place the sole of your right foot on the receiver's left ankle. Then, with dynamic impetus, turn your hips and left foot to your right, push his right elbow up, and pull him around by the lapel with your right hand. Your right elbow is now down.

5▼ As he falls, use both your hands to turn him over so he falls on his back, and bring your right foot around to place it on the mat

TOP TIP
Make sure your supporting foot is turned to the right, to allow your hips to generate a strong turning movement away from your blocking leg.

6▶ Hold onto the receiver's arm with both hands as he makes a breakfall.

HOLDS

Basic scarf hold
Hon kesa gatame

Basic scarf hold is often the first holding technique taught to beginners, because it's easy to learn. Before attempting any of the holds in this section, please consult pages 106–7, How to Submit.

2▼ Clamp your partner's wrist in your armpit. Place your foot tightly against his side and come down to a kneeling position. Then, pass your left hand under his arm to grasp his jacket. Begin to reach forwards with your right arm, towards his neck.

1▲ From standing, with your partner having just taken a breakfall, retain the tension on his arm and bring his hand across towards your left armpit, your leg against his side.

TOP TIP
Coordinate moving your leg under your partner's arm in step 3, with the turn of your body and head, to establish tight contact between the upper bodies and increase the pressure against the chest.

3▼ Take hold of the receiver's collar and move your right leg under his right arm. With the hand that's holding his sleeve, take up the slack in the material. This will give you added control of the arm as you turn your body and head to the left to bring the side of your chest into firm contact with his chest.

4◄ Take control, keeping your hip low, and bring your right leg all the way forwards. There should be no gaps between your bodies. With your right hand, hold the receiver's collar on the far side of his neck, your forearm keeping his head off the mat. This will prevent him from using a bridging action in an attempt to escape. For added control, bend your left leg, keeping your foot on the mat.

Side view

Broken scarf hold
Kzure kesa gatame

Broken scarf hold is more of a contest technique than basic scarf hold. The modified placement of the right arm is often quicker and easier to achieve, as is transferring to another technique.

TOP TIP
If the receiver attempts an escape by turning to his left, causing you to roll across him, release the hand holding his shoulder. Then move this hand further out and place it on the mat to brace against the movement.

1▼ With your partner lying flat on his back, hold his right arm in tension with both your hands on his sleeve.

2▼ Go down onto your left knee, with your right leg bent and against your partner's side. Take his right hand into your left armpit and clamp it at the wrist. With your left hand, grasp the under-arm part of his sleeve.

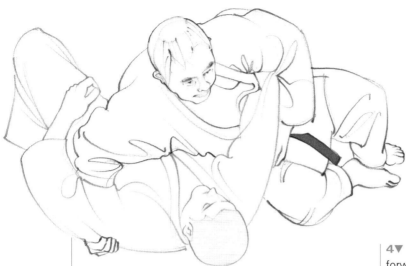

3▲ Lower the side of your chest onto your partner's front. Move your right arm over his body and between his arm and side. Place your right thigh on the mat. Grasp the material at his left shoulder and clamp his right arm against your chest, taking up the slack of his sleeve material with your left hand.

4▼ Bring your right foot well forwards and drop your left knee to the mat to complete the technique, clamping the receiver's body tightly. Your right knee (now positioned under the right shoulder) combines with your strong body tension and the hand holding the left shoulder, to prevent his head from pushing down on the mat in an attempt to bridge out of the hold.

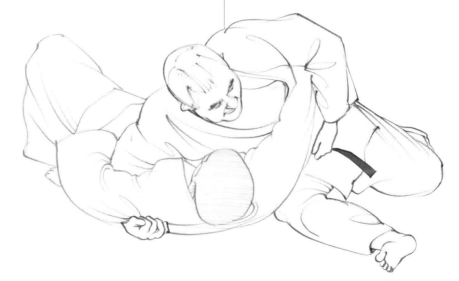

Upper-four-quarters hold
Kami shiho katame

Upper-four-quarters hold is very effective. It's used here to demonstrate the basic principles of control, contact and body management.

TOP TIP
When practising this technique, the receiver should turn his head to the side to avoid uncomfortable pressure on the face. In a contest situation, discomfort may be accepted in the heat of battle!

1▼ With your partner lying on his back, kneel close to his head. Place your hands palms down on the mat and slide them under his shoulders. Note that your partner remains alert and in a stable posture, involving himself in the practice.

2▼ Moving your upper body forwards, bring your chest into contact with your partner's chest, sliding your hands forward towards his belt. Keep your arms pressed tight against your partner.

3▼ Turning your hands up to grasp the belt, make tight contact with the receiver, using your chest. To achieve further control, press your abdomen against his head and clamp your elbows against his shoulders. Expect your partner to plan an escape strategy – for example, he may place his hands in contact with you, preparing to push, pull or turn.

4▼ To stabilize your position and prevent your partner from twisting you over and escaping, straighten your legs out behind you and take a wider stance. Angle your toes outwards and push down; this will aid body tension and allow you to respond energetically to any escape attempt.

Broken upper-four-quarters hold
Kzure kami shiho gatame

Broken upper-four-quarters hold is used in two common ways. This version involves a grip on the collar from underneath the shoulder; the other has the focus on the belt.

TOP TIP
Take advantage of the rule that prohibits pushing the face. Look towards your partner's free hand, which, if you turned away, he could use to push the back of your head – a move that would be permitted.

1▼ Kneeling on your right knee to the side of your partner's head, with your left knee raised, take his left hand and place it into your armpit to clamp the wrist.

2▼ Take his collar with your right hand. Then pull upwards to make a space for your left hand to slide underneath the shoulder and grasp the back of the collar. Wrap your left arm firmly around the receiver's as you lower your body.

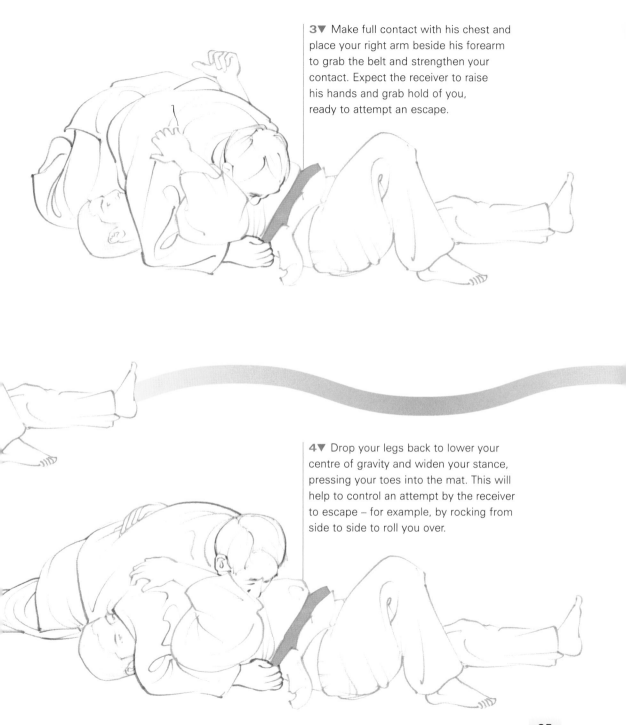

3▼ Make full contact with his chest and place your right arm beside his forearm to grab the belt and strengthen your contact. Expect the receiver to raise his hands and grab hold of you, ready to attempt an escape.

4▼ Drop your legs back to lower your centre of gravity and widen your stance, pressing your toes into the mat. This will help to control an attempt by the receiver to escape – for example, by rocking from side to side to roll you over.

Shoulder hold
Kata gatame

Shoulder hold is a comfortable technique to perform – but uncomfortable to receive! The version shown here is very stable. Unlike most other holds, there is no direct chest-to-chest contact.

1▶ Kneel alongside your partner, with your right foot in contact with his side. Using both hands, take hold of his arm at the wrist.

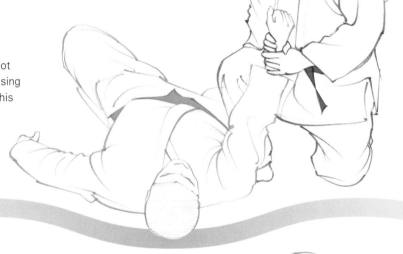

2▶ Keeping your right hand on his wrist, move your left hand to the receiver's arm, just above the elbow. Lean forwards to push his arm across his face. Your right knee should contact the side of his chest.

> **TOP TIP**
> Ensure that you maintain control from start to finish. It's important that you don't take your hands away from the arm until it's under the firm control of your head and body.

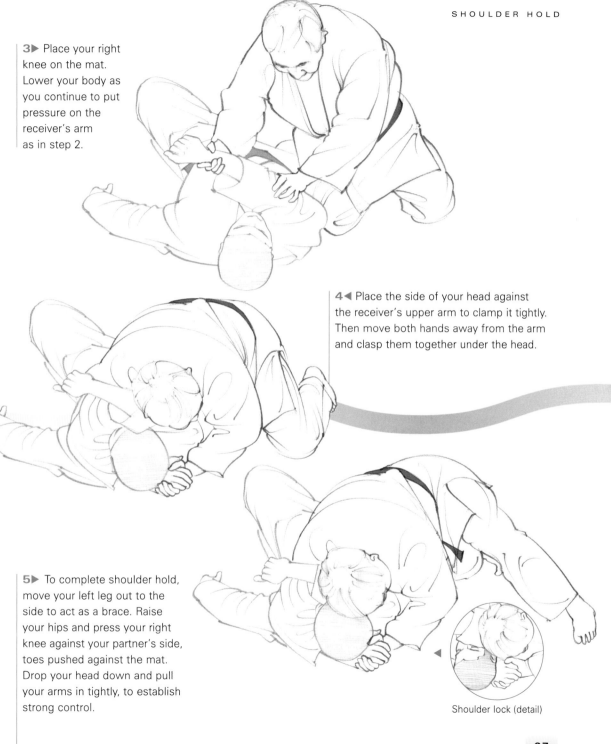

3▶ Place your right knee on the mat. Lower your body as you continue to put pressure on the receiver's arm as in step 2.

4◀ Place the side of your head against the receiver's upper arm to clamp it tightly. Then move both hands away from the arm and clasp them together under the head.

5▶ To complete shoulder hold, move your left leg out to the side to act as a brace. Raise your hips and press your right knee against your partner's side, toes pushed against the mat. Drop your head down and pull your arms in tightly, to establish strong control.

Shoulder lock (detail)

67

Combination (1)

Here, basic scarf hold is combined with shoulder hold. This combination demonstrates how an escape attempt from your opponent can enable you to change to a different hold while retaining control.

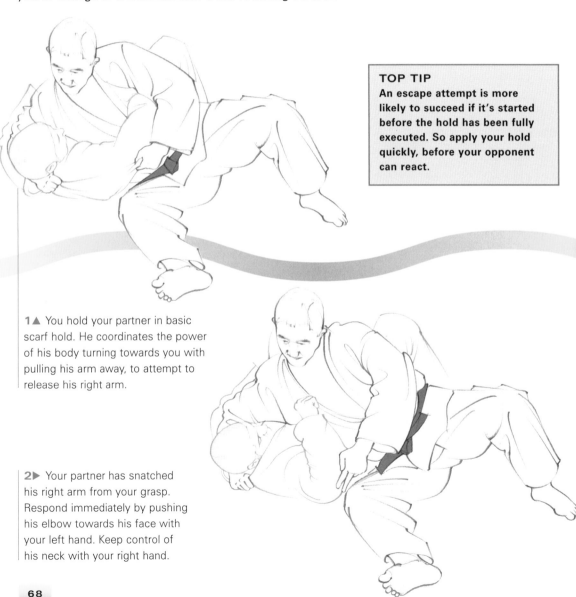

1▲ You hold your partner in basic scarf hold. He coordinates the power of his body turning towards you with pulling his arm away, to attempt to release his right arm.

2▶ Your partner has snatched his right arm from your grasp. Respond immediately by pushing his elbow towards his face with your left hand. Keep control of his neck with your right hand.

3▶ Bend your left arm around so that your hand points to your partner's left. Keep pushing his elbow with your hand while you transfer your weight to enable your head to take over control of the arm.

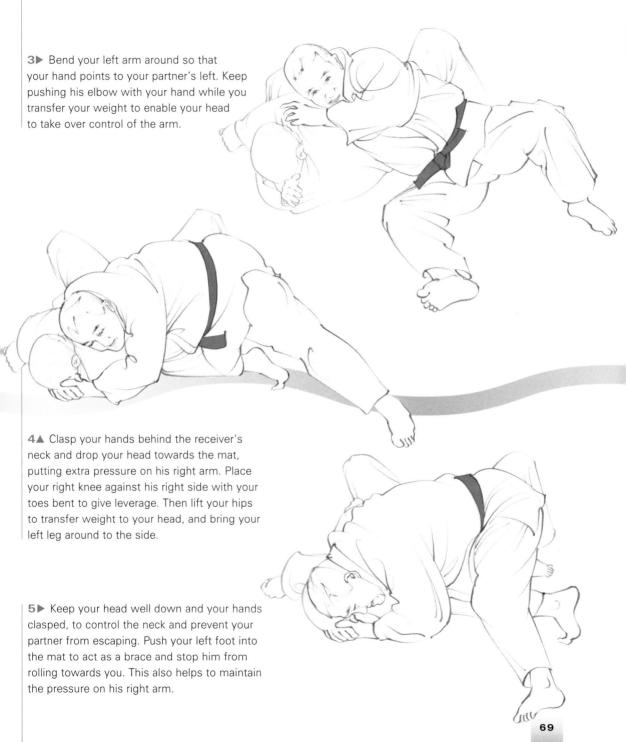

4▲ Clasp your hands behind the receiver's neck and drop your head towards the mat, putting extra pressure on his right arm. Place your right knee against his right side with your toes bent to give leverage. Then lift your hips to transfer weight to your head, and bring your left leg around to the side.

5▶ Keep your head well down and your hands clasped, to control the neck and prevent your partner from escaping. Push your left foot into the mat to act as a brace and stop him from rolling towards you. This also helps to maintain the pressure on his right arm.

Combination (2)

Broken scarf hold is used here with side four-quarters hold (yoko shiho gatame), to show how the receiver can exploit the weak point of a technique to escape, and how you can regain the initiative by changing your position.

TOP TIP
In step 5, smaller people may hold onto the lower part of the jacket or the trouser leg; larger people may be able to reach the belt. It's important that the chest stays over the receiver's upper body to prevent him sitting up. Use your hand to control the neck.

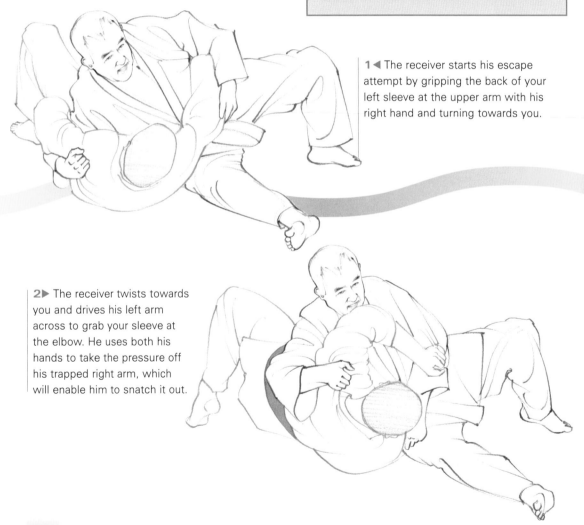

1 ◄ The receiver starts his escape attempt by gripping the back of your left sleeve at the upper arm with his right hand and turning towards you.

2 ► The receiver twists towards you and drives his left arm across to grab your sleeve at the elbow. He uses both his hands to take the pressure off his trapped right arm, which will enable him to snatch it out.

3▼ Twist towards your partner and bring your left hand across to grasp his collar underneath the neck. Rolling your left shoulder forwards, drop your chest towards him to control his arm.

4▶ Take your right leg to your right and bring your left leg forwards, so that your hips turn and your chest comes into full contact with the receiver. Control his left arm and neck with your head and right arm; use your left arm to control the other side of his neck. Position your left leg so that your thigh and knee control his right arm. Flex your toes and push them into the mat to keep the pressure forwards.

5◀ Bring your right arm between and underneath the receiver's legs to grasp the jacket by his left hip. Draw your right leg in to maintain stability and control. Holding the jacket at the collar and hip, stretch the material taut.

Combination (3)

This sequence shows upper-four-quarters hold combined with rear scarf hold (ushiro kesa gatame). The person executing the technique responds to an escape attempt by changing his hold. At no point is the holding cancelled, even though the hold has altered.

1▼ You hold your partner in upper four-quarters hold, but the hold is not yet fully secured as you haven't dropped your hips. The receiver prepares to take advantage of this in order to escape.

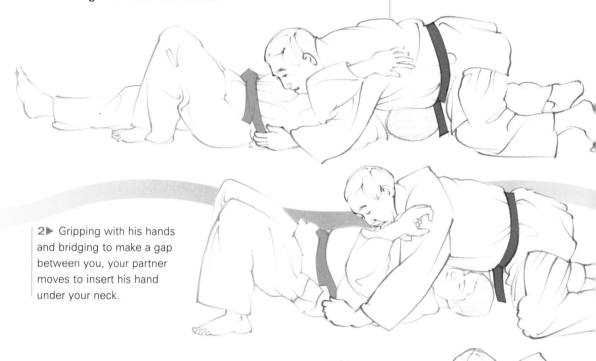

2▶ Gripping with his hands and bridging to make a gap between you, your partner moves to insert his hand under your neck.

3▶ Pull on his belt with both hands and bring your head and upper chest down. This stops the receiver from bringing his arm under your chin and linking his hands together. If he does manage to do this, he can use the power of both arms to push you away.

TOP TIP
If you are being held, bring your legs in with your knees raised. Push on the mat with both feet to lift your hips and get more power into pushing your opponent away.

Belt lock (detail)

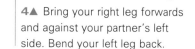

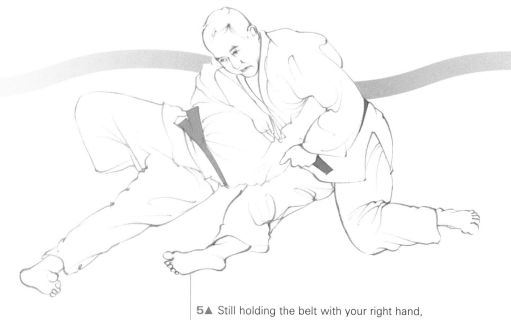

4▲ Bring your right leg forwards and against your partner's left side. Bend your left leg back.

5▲ Still holding the belt with your right hand, release your left hand in order to clamp your partner's left wrist in your armpit and hold his jacket. Keep your legs stretched out in a wide stance to complete rear scarf hold.

GROUNDWORK

Groundwork
Turnover techniques

When going into groundwork your partner may take up a defensive position, and you need to be able to deal with this. Here are two basic ways to turn your opponent onto their back to control them.

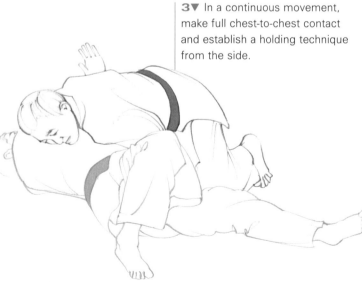

2▲ Pull his arm towards your hip, and, as you do so, use your shoulder to push his shoulder across and down. This will force his left shoulder to curve inwards. Continue to push your body forwards to roll your partner onto his back.

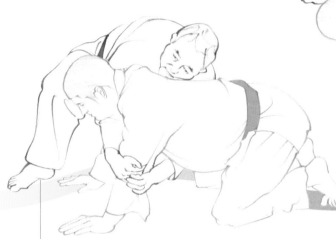

ALL-FOURS TURNOVER
1▲ If your partner is on all fours, place one arm underneath his chin and the other across his chest. With both hands, grasp his elbow and pull. With your head, push down on his back and chest to prevent him from escaping.

3▼ In a continuous movement, make full chest-to-chest contact and establish a holding technique from the side.

FACE-DOWN TURNOVER

1▶ This is useful if your partner is lying on his front with his hands underneath his chin to guard against a strangle. Take a firm grip on his judogi at the hip and the elbow.

2◀ With a fast snatching movement, use your arms and your back and hip muscles to roll your partner towards you and onto his back.

3▶ As soon as your partner is on his back, take full control by applying a hold. This turnover technique relies on explosive action for effect and, applied correctly, even very heavy opponents can be turned over.

Attack from between opponent's legs (1)

Being trapped between your opponent's legs puts you in a very weak position; it's nearly impossible to apply a technique against them in this situation, and they can use their legs to control you. This sequence ends with the receiver in broken scarf hold.

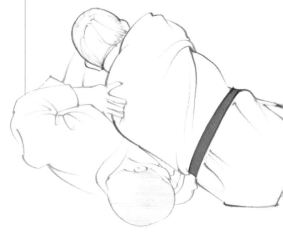

2▲ Kneel down on your left knee and drop your left shoulder to make contact with his upper body, maintaining your grip on the legs. Expect him to try to push you away.

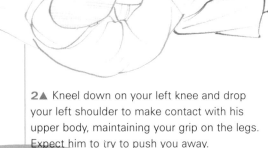

3▼ Lower your hips and roll backwards towards the head – this effectively blocks his arms. To assist the body-turn and stabilize your control, drive your left leg forwards, underneath the right, and swing your right leg back towards your partner's head.

1▲ Grasp the material inside of and just above your partner's knees. Push sideways and down with your left hand, and use your right to stop him from pushing inwards with his leg. Move from between his legs, stepping over with your left leg, then your right.

TOP TIP
Make sure you grip the trouser material firmly and tightly around both thighs by taking up the slack.

4▲ Releasing your right-hand grip on his knee, turn towards the receiver and make firm chest-to-chest contact. Pass your right hand under his left shoulder to grab the jacket. Release your left hand in preparation to clamp his right arm.

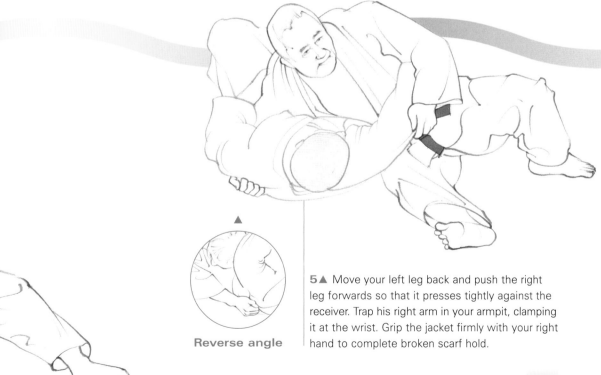

▲

Reverse angle

5▲ Move your left leg back and push the right leg forwards so that it presses tightly against the receiver. Trap his right arm in your armpit, clamping it at the wrist. Grip the jacket firmly with your right hand to complete broken scarf hold.

Attack from between opponent's legs (2)

If your opponent clamps your leg between his, you will need to escape before you can apply a technique. It's important that you make your move as soon as your leg is restricted, before your opponent settles. This sequence demonstrates how to escape and then apply lateral four-quarters hold (tatae shiho gatame).

1▶ Straighten the knee of your trapped leg and push on your partner's left knee with your right hand to loosen the contact, so that you can move yourself up his body.

2▼ Push your head forwards to control his arm. Make close contact with his upper body, your hands holding his suit underneath to gain complete control of his head and shoulders.

4▶ With your legs each side of the receiver, establish full chest-to-chest contact. Place your left forearm under and around his neck. Use your head to press his upper arm against his head.

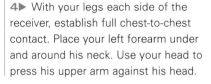

TOP TIP
When you push on the receiver's leg and free your own leg in step 3, apply the actions simultaneously and with impulse energy – a quick coordinated movement.

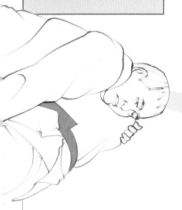

5▼ Clasp your hands together and trap the receiver's arm with your head, to make tight contact with him. Position your heels underneath the thighs so that you gain total control, and complete lateral four-quarters hold.

3▲ Release your right hand and push on your partner's knee. You are now in a more effective position than you were in step 1, so you should be able to loosen his contact enough to free your leg. Step beside his left thigh.

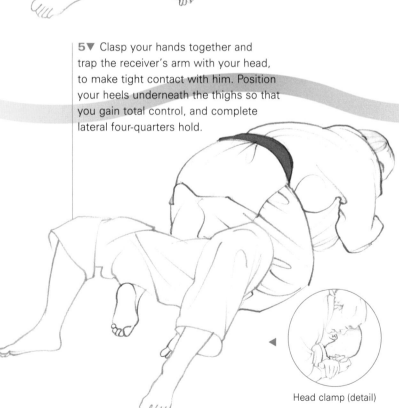

Head clamp (detail)

From standing to holding

Progressing from a standing technique to groundwork is a good way to experience the essence of a Judo contest – a continuous flow leading to a satisfactory conclusion. It's up to you to take control and maintain the initiative from beginning to end.

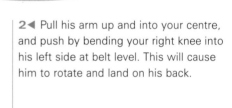

1▶ Your partner is on all fours. He passes his right arm under his body for you to take with both hands. Stand with your right knee in contact with his left side.

2◀ Pull his arm up and into your centre, and push by bending your right knee into his left side at belt level. This will cause him to rotate and land on his back.

TOP TIP
Steps 1 to 3 make a good exercise for improving your breakfalls, simulating a side breakfall from a standing technique. Make sure you practise to both sides.

3◄ By maintaining good posture and keeping hold of the arm, you will keep control and help your partner to make a good breakfall. As he does so, prepare for your groundwork technique by clamping his wrist in your left armpit and start moving into basic scarf hold.

4▼ Maintain the scarf-hold technique, taking care not to fall onto the receiver with force. Establish contact firmly and keep control throughout.

Reverse angle

5► Drop your head forwards to transfer your weight onto his upper body and prevent him from sitting up and making an escape. Be aware, however, that the receiver is still able to grip your belt, so could attempt an alternative escape.

83

Escape from basic scarf hold

This sequence shows how to escape from basic scarf hold, and then reverse the initiative to hold the receiver with broken scarf hold. Applying the alternative form of scarf hold in this way prevents them from using the same escape and reversal.

> **TOP TIP**
> In step 2, if your opponent pushes back you should pull; if they pull away then push – going with the flow is an important Judo principle.

1▶ You are held by your partner with basic scarf hold. Place your arms around her and take hold of her belt with both hands. Then start to push her away to begin your escape.

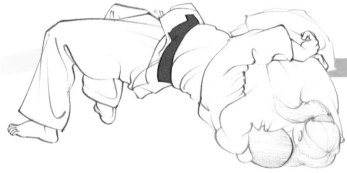

2◀ With a strong bridging movement, twist to your right, gripping your partner's belt, to lift her hips off the mat. Here, she attempts to regain the initiative by rolling back. (If the receiver doesn't respond, she can be pushed all the way over onto her front, to cancel her hold.)

3▶ Drop to the mat and take advantage of the gap you've created by pushing your body underneath your partner. Pull on her belt to keep close contact, and start to roll to your left, taking her with you.

4▶ Straighten your left leg outwards and push your right foot into the mat to assist the turn, rolling the receiver over your chest with a strong hip rotation.

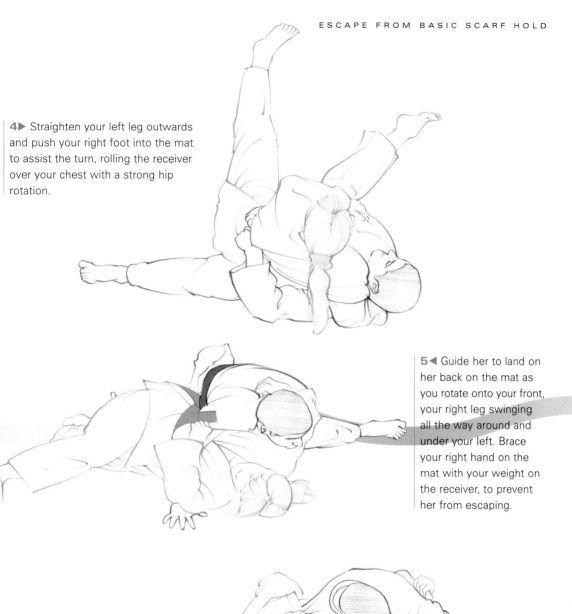

5◀ Guide her to land on her back on the mat as you rotate onto your front, your right leg swinging all the way around and under your left. Brace your right hand on the mat with your weight on the receiver, to prevent her from escaping.

6▶ Take control of your partner's right arm by trapping her wrist in your armpit and holding the sleeve tightly. Grip her jacket at the shoulder and bring your right leg far forwards to complete broken scarf hold.

Escape from broken scarf hold

This sequence demonstrates how you can exploit the weakness in a hold. Your opponent won't wait around while you attempt your escape, so you must move with energy and speed to unsettle your opponent. Here, the escape is from broken scarf hold.

TOP TIP
When you feel confident enough, try continuing from this sequence into side four-quarters hold. Learning to move from one technique to another is a crucial part of the Judo experience.

1◄ Press down on the mat with your left foot and turn towards your trapped right arm, placing your left forearm under your partner's chin.

2▼ Grasping his jacket with both hands, push and pull his arm to relieve the pressure on your right arm.

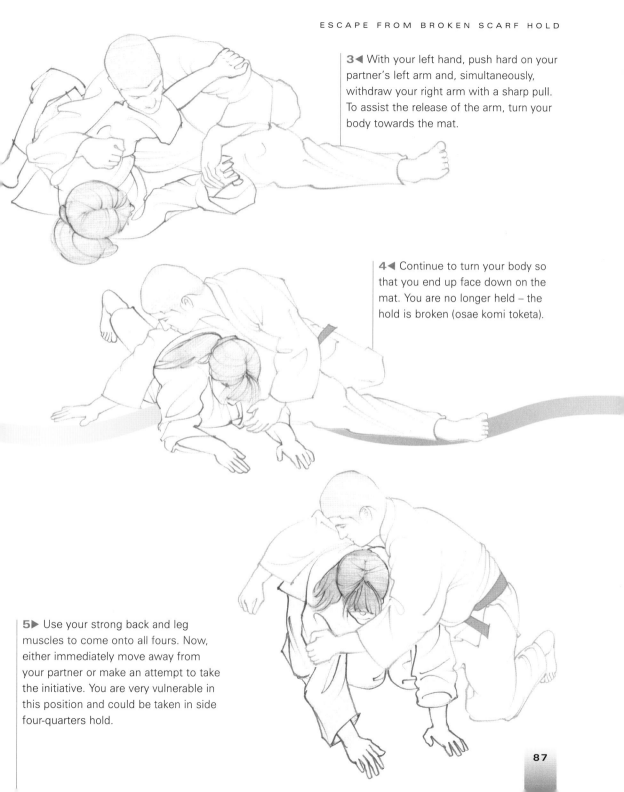

3◄ With your left hand, push hard on your partner's left arm and, simultaneously, withdraw your right arm with a sharp pull. To assist the release of the arm, turn your body towards the mat.

4◄ Continue to turn your body so that you end up face down on the mat. You are no longer held – the hold is broken (osae komi toketa).

5▶ Use your strong back and leg muscles to come onto all fours. Now, either immediately move away from your partner or make an attempt to take the initiative. You are very vulnerable in this position and could be taken in side four-quarters hold.

Escape from broken upper-four-quarters hold

This sequence demonstrates an escape from broken upper-four-quarters hold, using strong bridging and twisting movements of your body to unsettle your opponent.

1▼ As soon as you are held in broken upper-four-quarters hold and before your opponent is settled, start to escape by bridging.

2▼ Bridging up strongly, reach over to hold your partner's belt with your left hand, and twist your body towards your right.

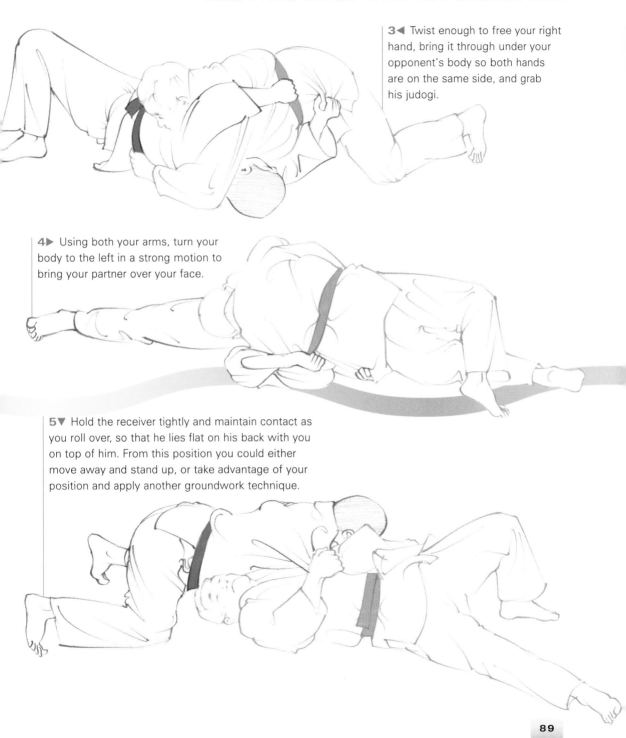

3◄ Twist enough to free your right hand, bring it through under your opponent's body so both hands are on the same side, and grab his judogi.

4► Using both your arms, turn your body to the left in a strong motion to bring your partner over your face.

5▼ Hold the receiver tightly and maintain contact as you roll over, so that he lies flat on his back with you on top of him. From this position you could either move away and stand up, or take advantage of your position and apply another groundwork technique.

Escape from shoulder hold

This is a good example of body management (*tai sabaki*) as it shows continuous coordinated movement. Practise the sequence as an exercise to find the best way to use your effort to maximum effect.

1◄ You are held in shoulder hold, with your head, neck and right upper arm strongly controlled. Clasp your hands together and push your right elbow against the side of your partner's neck to loosen her control on you.

2▼ Turn in and drop your right knee to the mat, sliding it along to make contact with the receiver. Reach across with your left hand to grab her belt, and grip her sleeve at the upper arm with your right.

3► Grip her belt tightly with your left hand, and grab her right upper arm with your right hand. Using your legs, hips, shoulders and head in a powerful coordinated movement, bring her across your body and onto the mat, so that she lands on her back.

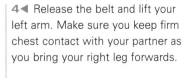

4◀ Release the belt and lift your left arm. Make sure you keep firm chest contact with your partner as you bring your right leg forwards.

5▼ With your right hand, guide the receiver's right arm towards your left armpit. Clamp the arm and grasp the sleeve, establishing a tight hold with your left arm before you let go with your right hand. Place your feet wide apart to establish a firm base.

TOP TIP
To loosen your partner's control, push up from your left leg and raise your hip, turning your body inwards to combine the power from your centre with the push from your arms, to press your elbow against her.

6▶ Take your right arm around the receiver's neck, lifting her head. Your right knee, hip and side should make contact with her body. Move your left foot back and keep your right knee bent. Lift your head as you firmly grip the right arm.

Escape from side four-quarters hold

In this sequence the receiver of side four-quarters hold escapes, and then retrieves the initiative by applying broken upper-four-quarters hold. In this version of the hold, you gain control by clamping one arm under the armpit and passing the other arm under the opposite shoulder to grip the belt.

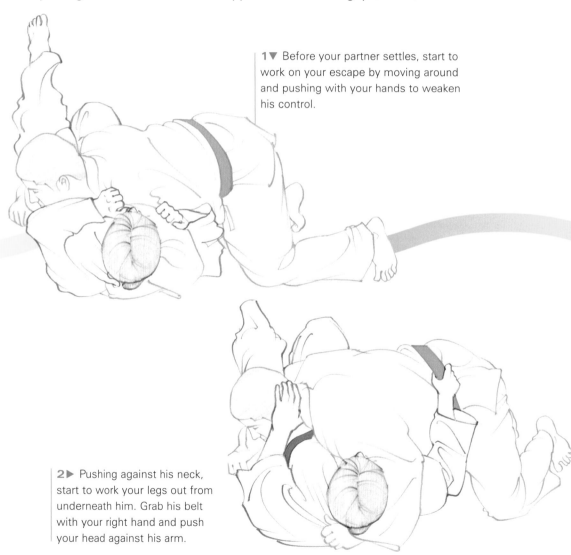

1▼ Before your partner settles, start to work on your escape by moving around and pushing with your hands to weaken his control.

2▶ Pushing against his neck, start to work your legs out from underneath him. Grab his belt with your right hand and push your head against his arm.

3▼ In a coordinated movement, push your right foot to the left, as shown, and use the strength in your hips to rotate towards your partner and work yourself free, bringing your head towards his middle.

TOP TIP
When you've turned your partner over, slide your body back towards his upper torso. If you don't keep your weight over your partner's upper body, he'll sit up and escape.

4▼ Hooking your left leg around the receiver's head, turn him onto his back by combining pushing and turning movements. If necessary, push your right hand against the mat to assist. This is a continuous action.

5▼ Settling on the receiver's upper body, clamp his right arm between your knee and arm. Grip his jacket firmly and maintain firm contact with the chest. Push your left arm under his left shoulder to grasp the belt. Hold it tightly.

STRANGLES

Naked strangle
Hadaka jime

In Judo there is no distinction between a strangle and a choke. The technique shown here, naked strangle, demonstrates the principles of applying strangles (shime waza). Before attempting any of the techniques in this section, please consult pages 106–7, How to Submit.

> **WARNING**
> Strangles must be practised slowly and carefully, and should be used only if a qualified first-aider is nearby.

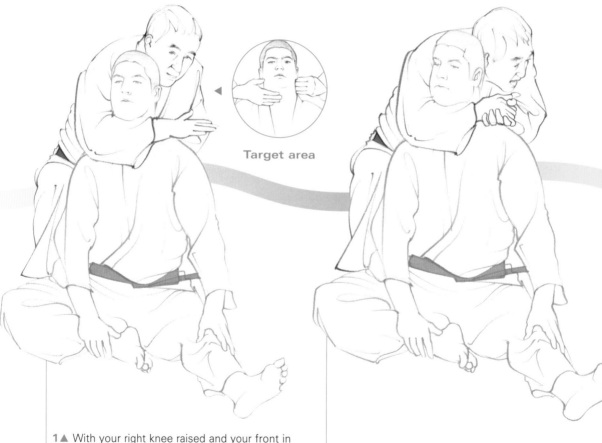

Target area

1▲ With your right knee raised and your front in contact with your partner's back, place your right arm across his throat with the bony part of the inner wrist in contact with the Adam's apple.

2▲ Clasp your hands together and place the side of your head against your partner's head, to establish close contact.

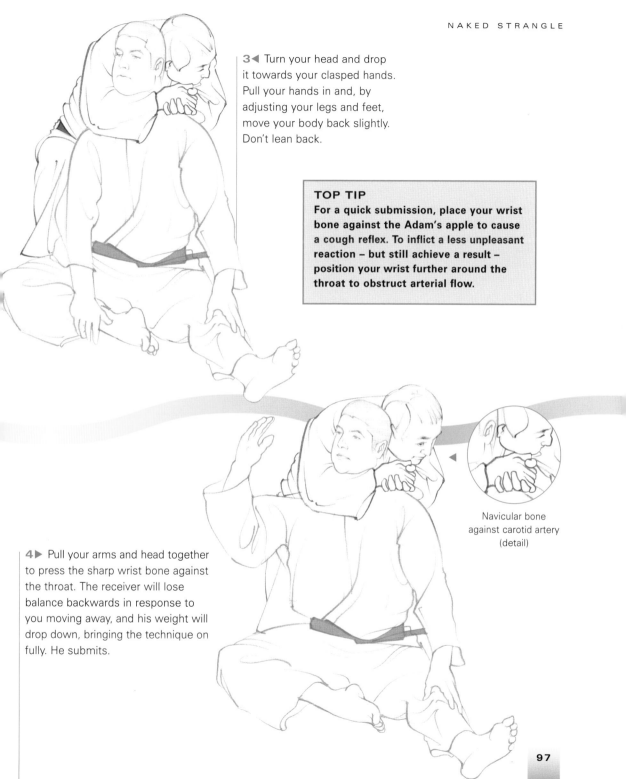

3◄ Turn your head and drop it towards your clasped hands. Pull your hands in and, by adjusting your legs and feet, move your body back slightly. Don't lean back.

TOP TIP
For a quick submission, place your wrist bone against the Adam's apple to cause a cough reflex. To inflict a less unpleasant reaction – but still achieve a result – position your wrist further around the throat to obstruct arterial flow.

Navicular bone against carotid artery (detail)

4▶ Pull your arms and head together to press the sharp wrist bone against the throat. The receiver will lose balance backwards in response to you moving away, and his weight will drop down, bringing the technique on fully. He submits.

Sliding lapel strangle
Okuri eri jime

Sliding lapel strangle works by obstructing the flow of blood to the brain, resulting in deprivation of oxygen and, if no submission is given, unconsciousness. When practising any strangle, apply the technique slowly and carefully.

1 ▼ Raise your right knee, placing it against your partner's back. Pull his left lapel aside and insert your right hand around the neck, grabbing deep inside the right collar.

2 ▼ Release the left lapel and reach across to take hold of the right lapel, pulling it taut. Take up the slack in the collar with your right hand and pull your elbow back.

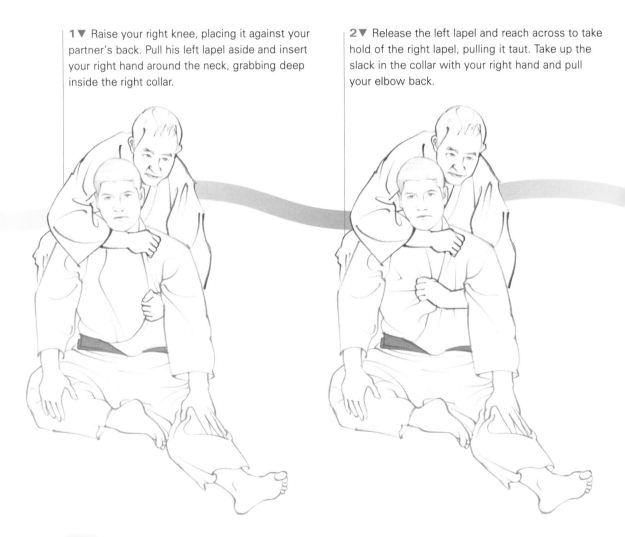

3◄ Maintain a firm grip with your left hand and withdraw your right leg and shoulder, pulling your right arm back with the hand gripping firmly to tighten the receiver's left collar around his neck.

4▼ As soon as your partner feels the strangle taking effect, he should tap in submission.

WARNING
When oxygen is restricted by pressure on the carotid artery, unconsciousness can occur suddenly within a few seconds. It's vital that the receiver submits as soon as the effects are felt. When performing the technique, you must be prepared to release your partner even if they don't submit, should you suspect they're losing consciousness.

JOINT LOCKS

Cross armlock
Ude hishigi juji gatame

Cross armlock (popularly called 'juji gatame') is a joint lock (kansetsu waza). Judo originally included locks against the knees, hips and wrists, but modern Judo practised as a sport only allows elbow locks. These are said to be less dangerous as pain is felt before damage, allowing time for submission. Before attempting any of the joint locks in this section, please consult pages 106–7, How to Submit.

1▶ With your partner lying on his back, kneel on your left knee with your right foot against his right-hand side. Now hold his right wrist with both hands, ready to take control.

WARNING
Joint locks must be applied slowly and carefully; submit as soon as pain is felt, and be cautious about repetitive use. Children and young adults may be particularly at risk from these techniques as the bones and joints are still developing.

TOP TIP
Practise getting your left foot in quickly, stepping over or smoothly around the head, positioning the foot accurately and flowing into the next stage.

2▶ Moving closer, place your right knee on the receiver's chest, tight against the armpit.

3◀ Holding his hand and arm close to your body, keep your knee over his chest. Then rise up and lean forwards, placing your left leg tight against your partner's head and left shoulder.

4▼ With your knees together to clamp the receiver's arm, drop onto your back. Keep your knees bent so that you maintain close contact with him, and can control his head and upper body to prevent him turning out of the technique.

5▼ With both hands, hold onto your partner's outstretched arm, palm facing up. Clamp his elbow tightly between your knees. Then pull the arm towards you and raise your hips slightly, to cause his elbow joint to overextend. Immediately, he will feel the effects of the technique, and submit.

Wrist-grab (detail)

Figure four armlock
Ude garame

This sequence demonstrates a figure four armlock, or arm entanglement, being applied in response to an escape attempt from broken scarf hold.

WARNING
Take extra care when applying this type of technique as your body weight and momentum are employed against the receiver's relatively weak arm structure.

1▲ The receiver turns towards you and pushes his left arm across in an attempt to escape. His arm is bent at the elbow to enable him to push under your chin.

3▲ Continue to turn until you're chest to chest with your partner. Slide your right arm under his bent elbow so that you can grasp your other wrist. Keep his hand on the mat, and increase the torsion on the elbow by sliding your hands inwards until he submits.

TOP TIP
Practise coordinating the action of linking your hands to develop an affective arm-entanglement technique.

2▶ As your partner attempts to push, catch his wrist and push it back to the mat, turning your left shoulder towards him. The receiver may actually aid this action by trying to pull his wrist from your grip.

Armpit hold armlock
Waki gatame

The next sequence shows an alternative response to the same kind of escape attempt.

1▼ As your partner begins to straighten his arm to push across you, take advantage of the direction of the push by grabbing his wrist and pulling the arm. To aid the pull, start to turn your body to the left.

Wrist-grab (detail)

2▶ From a sitting position, keeping your partner's right arm straight, clamp the arm in your armpit. Grasp his arm and wrist with both hands, preparing to apply the armpit hold.

3▶ With your back leaning against the receiver, slide your backside forwards and pull him over onto his front. Adjust your grip on his hand so the palm faces up, then drop your head backwards and raise his hand to hyperextend the elbow. The receiver will submit.

105

Before using any grappling techniques – holds, strangles or joint locks – it's vital that you know how to submit, and have practised using the various techniques. It's also important that you are prepared to submit without hesitation to avoid being injured, if you are certain that an arm lock or strangle is taking effect. When you are applying a technique, you *must* respond immediately to a submission from your partner, by releasing them.

▲ WHEN FACE DOWN
If you are unable to tap the body, you should slap the mat at least twice with the palm of your hand, to give an audible signal of submission.

▲ WHEN YOUR HANDS ARE FREE Tap your partner at least twice on the body, using the palm of your free hand. A single tap may be confused with an escape attempt, so your partner would ignore this.

TOP TIP
Always tap your opponent's body to submit wherever possible. In the dojo, there are likely to be other noises that could mask the sound of you slapping the mat.

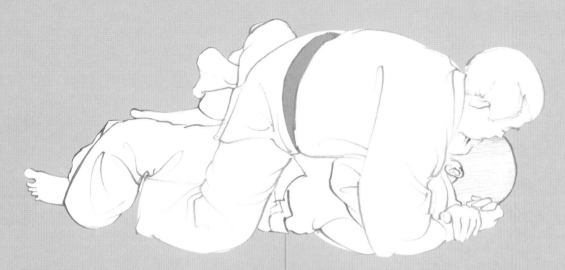

▲ **WHEN ALL LIMBS ARE TRAPPED** If you are unable to use your arms or legs to submit, then you should shout, '*Maitta*' (I submit) or just yell, 'I give up!'

▼ **WHEN YOUR HANDS ARE TRAPPED** If you can't use your arms to submit, you may give a signal using your legs, by slapping the mat with your feet more than once. It may also be possible to bring your knees up to tap your partner on the body.

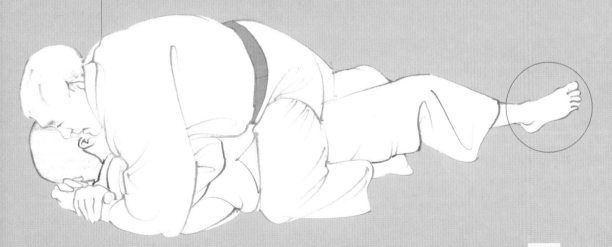

Training diary

Index of techniques

Please note:

Full demonstrations of the techniques are shown in **bold**.

About the author

Roger Marks, black belt 4th Dan, is registered with the British Judo Council. He started Judo in 1961 at the Budokwai martial arts and Judo club in London. His subsequent training was with Masutaro Otani 8th Dan who, as president of the BJC, awarded him his black belt, and Robin Otani, the current President and senior grade of the BJC.

Roger is a fully qualified coach and has been teaching since 1971. He holds a National Vocational Qualification for Sports Coaching in the context of Judo. He currently teaches Judo at MovingEast in London, where he also studies Aikido. For more information visit www.movingeast.co.uk.

About the consultant

Akinori Hosaka is graded 8th Dan by the Kodokan. His long Judo career started as a child in Japan, and continued throughout his time at Nihon University. He enjoyed a successful contest Judo career and was recommended by Saburo Matsushita to Trevor Leggett, who invited him to the UK to take up a three-year contract with Manchester KNK Judo Club.

Hosaka sensei has lived in the UK since 1962, where he has contributed a great deal to British Judo, including being National Squad Technical Coach for the British Judo Association, the UK leading body. He is currently Chief Examiner for the British Judo Council and Director of their Technical Centre for Excellence. He is also responsible for developing and establishing the Fundamental Principles of Judo certification courses for teachers. He has been the chief coach at the Sale Judo Club in Cheshire, UK, since 1972. Visit www.salejudo.com.

Acknowledgments

Thank you to the lovely people at Eddison Sadd Editions: Ian, Elaine, and Malcolm, for their constant support and guidance, and special thanks to Katie Golsby for translating my text from gibberish to English!

My sincere thanks to Akinori Hosaka sensei, for your remarkable patience and hard work in supervising and demonstrating the whole range of techniques. Many thanks also to Shahin Mehraban, 2nd Dan member of Sale Judo Club, for his modelling work and assistance, and to models Fay Goodman and Danielle Binnee.

Finally, thank you to the hundreds of Judo students I have taught and practised with and to those I will meet in the future – we learn from and teach each other.

EDDISON•SADD EDITIONS
Editorial Director Ian Jackson
Senior Editor Katie Golsby
Art Director Elaine Partington
Art Editor Malcolm Smythe
Illustrator Juliet Percival
Production Cara Herron

Eddison Sadd would like to thank all those who kindly took part in the reference photography.